How do people get to work? How do you get to school? On wheels of course! The wheels on cars, bicycles, trains and buses move you around.

Wheels rush fire engines to a fire. Wheels on a tractor help a farmer work in the fields. Special wheels are even used on the moon!

Bus

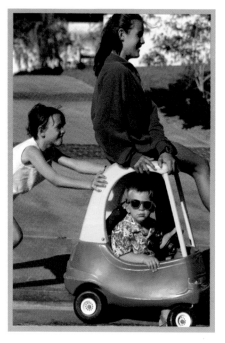

Buggy

A wheel is always shaped like a circle.

A wheel always moves round and round.

A wheel is used for moving things about – like the wheels on this little buggy.

Imagine a bicycle with no wheels – it could not move!

Bicycle

How does it move?

Skateboard

You use wheels all your life.
Wheels carry you around,
wheels carry your shopping –
and wheels can be fun!

6

Some things have more wheels than others. Which has more wheels – a pair of rollerblades or a skateboard?

Rollerblades

Beetle

Your feet push the pedals
on a bicycle. In a car, an engine
drives the wheels.

Cars are all
shapes and sizes.
The car above
looks like a beetle.

Family car

A sports car has a smooth body so it can go fast. A family car has a big boot to carry things in.

Sports car

School bus
Can you see the wheels?

A people mover can carry you, your family and your friends!

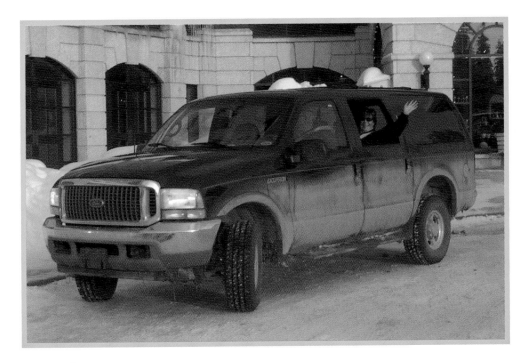

People mover

Buses and coaches carry even more people. Some have two decks so you can sit upstairs. Their wheels are very strong.

Train
Can you see the tracks?

Hundreds of people can ride on one train. Trains do not run on roads – their wheels run on railway tracks. The engine at the front pulls the coaches.

Trucks have lots of wheels to help them grip the road.

Can you count how many wheels are on this truck? Remember it has two sides.

Truck

The driver sits in the front part of the truck, called the cab.

This truck bends in the middle so that it can turn corners.

15

Some trucks have a special job like fire engines and ambulances. Fire engines are painted red so that it is easy to see them.

Ambulance

Fire engines and ambulances also flash their lights and make a loud howling noise. Their wheels are used day and night!

Fire engine

Sometimes a motorbike goes to the rescue!

Motorbike

Have you seen a digger with tracks? A track is like a long belt that rolls over lots of wheels.

Tracks help a digger grip the ground so it can push hard.

Tracks

Tractor

Tractors have big wheels so they do not sink into the ground.

Tyre

The thick tyres help the tractor grip in the slippery mud.

Dumper truck

This truck is as big as a house!

Its wheels are enormous, too.

Would you like to drive this truck? You have to climb up a ladder to get into the cab.

Big wheel

Some wheels are built for speed.

Look at these motorbikes go!

Motorbike race

Racing car

Racing cars travel so fast that their tyres wear out quickly.

A team changes the wheels by the side of the race track.

There are even wheels in space!

This buggy has wheels to ride across the surface of the moon.

Moon buggy

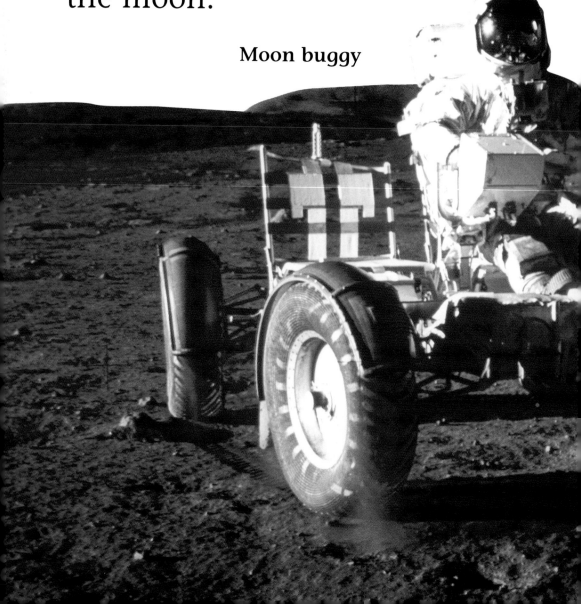

Space shuttles have wheels so they can land back on Earth.

Space shuttle

This machine on wheels has no driver – it is a rollercoaster. It rolls up, down and upside-down. Would you like a ride?

Rollercoaster

27

Can You Find?

This book is full of wheels – big and small, smooth and bumpy. Look at these wheels. Can you find them?

A

B

C

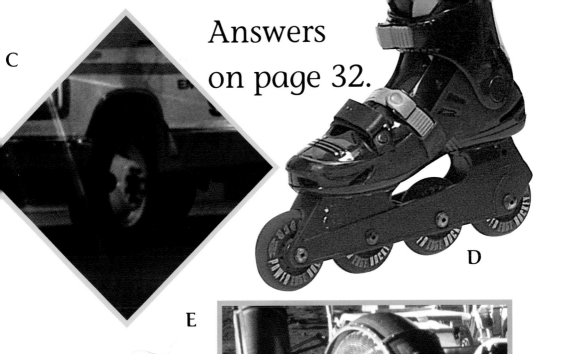

Answers
on page 32.

D

E

Clue: Look at
pages 5, 7, 14,
16, 19 and 24.

F

Do You Know?

People have been using wheels for thousands of years. Do you know what these wheels are made of?

Bicycle wheels

Stagecoach wheels

Car wheels

Train wheel

Spacecraft
wheels

Answers on page 32.

Index

ANSWERS TO QUESTIONS

Pages 28-29 – **A** comes from a bicycle • **B** comes from a tractor • **C** comes from an ambulance • **D** comes from a pair of rollerblades • **E** comes from a moon buggy • **F** comes from a truck.

Pages 30-31 – The first **bicycle wheels** were made of wood • **Stagecoach wheels** were made of wood • The first **car wheels** were made of wood • **Train wheels** are made of a metal called steel • **Spacecraft wheels** are made of light, strong metals.

Photocredits: Abbreviations: t-top, m-middle, b-bottom, r-right, l-left.
Cover, 1, 2ml, 2mr, 4, 5, 6, 12-13, 20, 21, 23, 26-27, 28l, 31mr - Digital Stock. 2tl, 7, 29tr - R. Vlitos. 2l, 3, 14-15, 29b - Scania. 8, 9 both, 11, 16-17, 22 - Select Pictures. 10, 16l, 29t - Corbis. 18 - John Deere. 19 both, 28r - Renault. 24, 25, 29mr - Stockbyte. 31b - NASA.
Illustrator: Peter Hutton, Alex Pang.